IN THIS ISSUE:

ISSUE 08 AUGUST 2017

PUBLISHER
Tourism Tattler (Pty) Ltd.
PO Box 891, Umhlanga Rocks, 4320
KwaZulu-Natal, South Africa.
Website: www.tourismtattler.com

EXECUTIVE EDITOR Des Langkilde
Cell: +27 (0)82 374 7260
Fax: +27 (0)86 651 8080
E-mail: editor@tourismtattler.com
Skype: tourismtattler

MAGAZINE ADVERTISING
ADVERTISING DIRECTOR Bev Langkilde
Cell: +27 (0)71 224 9971
Fax: +27 (0)86 656 3860
E-mail: bev@tourismtattler.com
Skype: bevtourismtattler

SUBSCRIPTIONS
http://eepurl.com/bocldD

BACK ISSUES (Click on the covers below).

▼ JUL 2017 ▼ JUN 2017 ▼ MAY 2017

▼ APR 2017 ▼ MAR 2017 ▼ FEB 2017
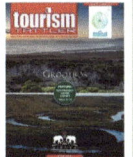  

▼ JAN 2017 ▼ DEC 2016 ▼ NOV 2016

▼ OCT 2016 ▼ SEP 2016 ▼ AUG 2016

CONTENTS

AFRICA'S SUSTAINABLE TOURISM GEMS
07 Mantis Collection

AFRICA: SUSTAINABLE TOURISM SOLUTIONS
09 EcoPlanet Bamboo
10 Eco & Sustainable Tourism Icons
11 Join the Fair Trade Move Toward Sustainability

ACCOLADES
12 World Luxury Spa Winners
14 World Luxury Restaurant Winners

BUSINESS & FINANCE
16 South African Tourism Statistics: Jan-May 2017
17 Global Tourism Statistics: Jan-Apr 2017
18 Economic Benefits of Hosting Events in Africa
19 Business Tourism in Africa Continues to Expand

DESTINATIONS
20 Discover Luxury in Kenya
24 South Africa's Ultimate Journey: 100 Worthy Places

EVENTS
27 THINC Africa Launches Business Meetings
28 Enabling Dealmaking at Travel Trade Events
29 Zimbabwe's Premium Travel Expo

LEGAL
31 The Consumer Goods & Services Ombudsman - Part 2

EDITORIAL CONTRIBUTORS
Des Langkilde — Martin Janse van Vuuren
Louis Nel — Zandre Campos

MAGAZINE SPONSORS
02 City Lodge Hotel Group
03 Bookings2Africa
05 Kenya Tourism Board
06 Zimbabwe Tourism Board
07 Mantis Group
08 World Luxury Spa & Restaurant Awards
09 EcoPlanet Bamboo
30 ATA Congress Rwanda 2017

SUPPORTED CHARITIES
32 Diabetes South Africa

Disclaimer: The Tourism Tattler is published by Tourism Tattler (Pty) Ltd and is the official trade journal of various trade 'associations' (see page 02). The Tourism Tattler digital e-zine, is distributed free of charge to bona fide tourism stakeholders. Letters to the Editor are assumed intended for publication in whole or part and may therefore be used for such purpose. The information provided and opinions expressed in this publication are provided in good faith and do not necessarily represent the opinions of Tourism Tattler (Pty) Ltd, its 'Associations', its staff and its production suppliers. Advice provided herein should not be soley relied upon as each set of circumstances may differ. Professional advice should be sought in each instance. Neither Tourism Tattler (Pty) Ltd, its 'Associations', its staff and its production suppliers can be held legally liable in any way for damages of any kind whatsoever arising directly or indirectly from any facts or information provided or omitted in these pages or from any statements made or withheld or from supplied photographs or graphic images reproduced by the publication.

List on Africa's dedicated booking portal

Accommodation
Adventure
Activities
Events
Tours

Bookings2Africa.com
Bringing Africa to the World and the World to Africa

 +27 (0)72 224 9971   www.bookings2africa.com   bev@bookings2africa.com

EDITORIAL
ACCREDITATION

Official Travel Trade Journal and Media Partner to:

The Africa Travel Association (ATA)
Tel: +1 212 447 1357 • Email: info@africatravelassociation.org • Website: www.africatravelassociation.org

ATA is a division of the Corporate Council on Africa (CCA), and a registered non-profit trade association in the USA, with headquarters in Washington, DC and chapters around the world. ATA is dedicated to promoting travel and tourism to Africa and strengthening intra-Africa partnerships. Established in 1975, ATA provides services to both the public and private sectors of the industry.

The African Travel & Tourism Association (Atta)
Tel: +44 20 7937 4408 • Email: info@atta.travel • Website: www.atta.travel

Members in 22 African countries and 37 worldwide use Atta to: Network and collaborate with peers in African tourism; Grow their online presence with a branded profile; Ask and answer specialist questions and give advice; and Attend key industry events.

National Accommodation Association of South Africa (NAA-SA)
Tel: +27 86 186 2272 • Fax: +2786 225 9858 • Website: www.naa-sa.co.za

The NAA-SA is a network of mainly smaller accommodation providers around South Africa – from B&Bs in country towns offering comfortable personal service to luxurious boutique city lodges with those extra special touches – you're sure to find a suitable place, and at the same time feel confident that your stay at an NAA-SA member's establishment will meet your requirements.

Regional Tourism Organisation of Southern Africa (RETOSA)
Tel: +27 11 315 2420/1 • Fax: +27 11 315 2422 • Website: www.retosa.co.za

RETOSA is a Southern African Development Community (SADC) institution responsible for tourism growth and development. RETOSA's aims are to increase tourist arrivals to the region through. RETOSA Member States are Angola, Botswana, DR Congo, Lesotho, Madagascar, Malawi, Mauritius, Mozambique, Namibia, Seychelles, South Africa, Swaziland, Tanzania, Zambia and Zimbabwe.

Southern African Vehicle Rental and Leasing Association (SAVRALA)
Contact: manager@savrala.co.za • Website: www.savrala.co.za

Founded in the 1970's, SAVRALA is the representative voice of Southern Africa's vehicle rental, leasing and fleet management sector. Our members have a combined national footprint with more than 600 branches countrywide. SAVRALA are instrumental in steering industry standards and continuously strive to protect both their members' interests, and those of the public, and are therefore widely respected within corporate and government sectors.

Seychelles Hospitality & Tourism Association (SHTA)
Tel: +248 432 5560 • Fax: +248 422 5718 • Website: www.shta.sc

The Seychelles Hospitality and Tourism Association was created in 2002 when the Seychelles Hotel Association merged with the Seychelles Hotel and Guesthouse Association. SHTA's primary focus is to unite all Seychelles tourism industry stakeholders under one association in order to be better prepared to defend the interest of the industry and its sustainability as the pillar of the country's economy.

International Coalition of Tourism Partners (ICTP)
Website: www.tourismpartners.org
ICTP is a travel and tourism coalition of global destinations committed to Quality Services and Green Growth.

International Institute for Peace through Tourism
Website: www.iipt.org
IIPT is dedicated to fostering tourism initiatives that contribute to international understanding and cooperation.

ITB Asia 2017
Website: www.itb-asia.com
25 to 27 October 2017 Marina Bay Sands®, Singapore.
ITB Asia is the leading B2B travel trade event for the entire Asia-Pacific region.

Tourism, Hotel Investment and Networking Conference 2017
Website: www.thincafrica..com
THINC Africa 2017 takes place in Cape Town, South Africa from 6-7 September.

The Hotel Show Africa 2017
Website: TheHotelShowAfrica.com
Thousands of hospitality professionals from around the world will be at Gallagher Convention Centre in Johannesburg from 25-27 June.

The Safari Awards
Website: www.safariawards.com
Safari Award finalists are amongst the top 3% in Africa and the winners are unquestionably the best.

SHWTE 2017
Website: SanganaiTourismExpo.com
27 Sep - 01 Oct at the Zimbabwe International Fair Grounds, Bulawayo.
The 2016 edition attracted: 212 Buyers, 236 Exhibitors, 3116 Meetings, and 5034 Connections.

World Luxury Hotel Awards
Website: www.luxuryhotelawards.com
World Luxury Hotel Awards is an international company that provides award recognition to the best hotels from all over the world.

Sanganai Hlanganani
WORLD TOURISM EXPO

"Africa's Premier Business Exchange"

27 September - 01 October 2017

CELEBRATING 10 years

ZIMBABWE INTERNATIONAL EXHIBITION CENTRE (ZIEC) BULAWAYO

Who should participate??

- National Tourism Boards
- Embassies
- Airlines
- Tourism destinations
- Tour Wholesalers, Tour Operators and Travel Agents
- Hotels
- Car Hire and Transport Operators
- Suppliers of goods and services to the tourism industry
- Investors
- Government Ministries
- Parastatals

#Sanganai2017

The fair will be filled with a lot of business and networking opportunities during exhibition hours and after hours, providing more opportunities to network.

DON'T MISS IT

Zimbabwe Tourism Authority
Tourism House, 55 Samora Machel Avenue
3rd Floor
tel: 263 4 780651/4, 752570, 758748, 774760
email: edson@ztazim.co.zw, sheona@ztazim.co.zw,
sanganai@ztazim.co.zw
website: www.sanganaitourismexpo.com

Zimbabwe *A World of Wonders*

OFFICIAL MEDIA PARTNER
tourism TATTLER
2017 INTERNATIONAL YEAR OF SUSTAINABLE TOURISM FOR DEVELOPMENT

ECO-FRIENDLY HOTELS & LODGES & ATTRACTIONS

Pearl Valley Lodges, South Africa

Oceana Beach and Wildlife Reserve, South Africa

Zambezi Queen, Namibia / Botswana

Founders Lodge by Mantis, South Africa

EcoPlanet Bamboo, South Africa

Mantis

The **Mantis Collection**, comprised of hotels, eco-escapes and lifestyle resorts, is deeply rooted in African conservation; with a vision for sustainability and a world in which people and animals co-exist.

Mantis is a family run collection of award winning, privately owned, five-star properties located around the World. Divided into five distinct groups, its specialist areas include Boutique Hotels, Game Reserves, Eco Lodges, Ski Lodges and Chalets and Yachts.

Officially founded by Adrian Gardiner in 2000, Mantis is committed to conservation and restoration, and each property is sensitive to its surroundings in respect of the building, environment and local community.

More recently, Mantis signed a Memorandum of Understanding with EcoPlanet Bamboo – a leader in the industrialization of bamboo as a commercial fibre through the restoration of degraded land by transforming it into sustainability certified global bamboo plantations. (See page 09).

EcoPlanet Bamboo and Mantis kick start this long term relationship with the utilization of a unique bamboo charcoal air purifier in all Mantis hotel rooms which is aimed at improving the quality of indoor air and reducing moisture in humid locations. The partnership will also introduce a specialized bamboo charcoal for the filtration of water, thereby reducing the use of plastic water bottles.

Short term commitments include moving the hotel collection's use of packaging for cosmetics, food and drinks to a renewable and compostable bamboo alternative, while the partnership's longer term commitment is to provide a tree-free, deforestation-free toilet paper. Eventually, Mantis aims to use EcoPlanet's bamboo fibre and clean pulping technology for the production of luxury textiles.

As a pioneer in the conservation of natural resources, this family run business is an inspiration for any entrepreneur.

Travel. Enjoy. Respect. #IYSTD17

QUICK LINKS:

- +27 (0)41 404 9300
- info@mantiscollection.com
- www.mantiscollection.com
- @MantisGroup
- @MantisGroup
- Mantis Collection
- MantisCollection

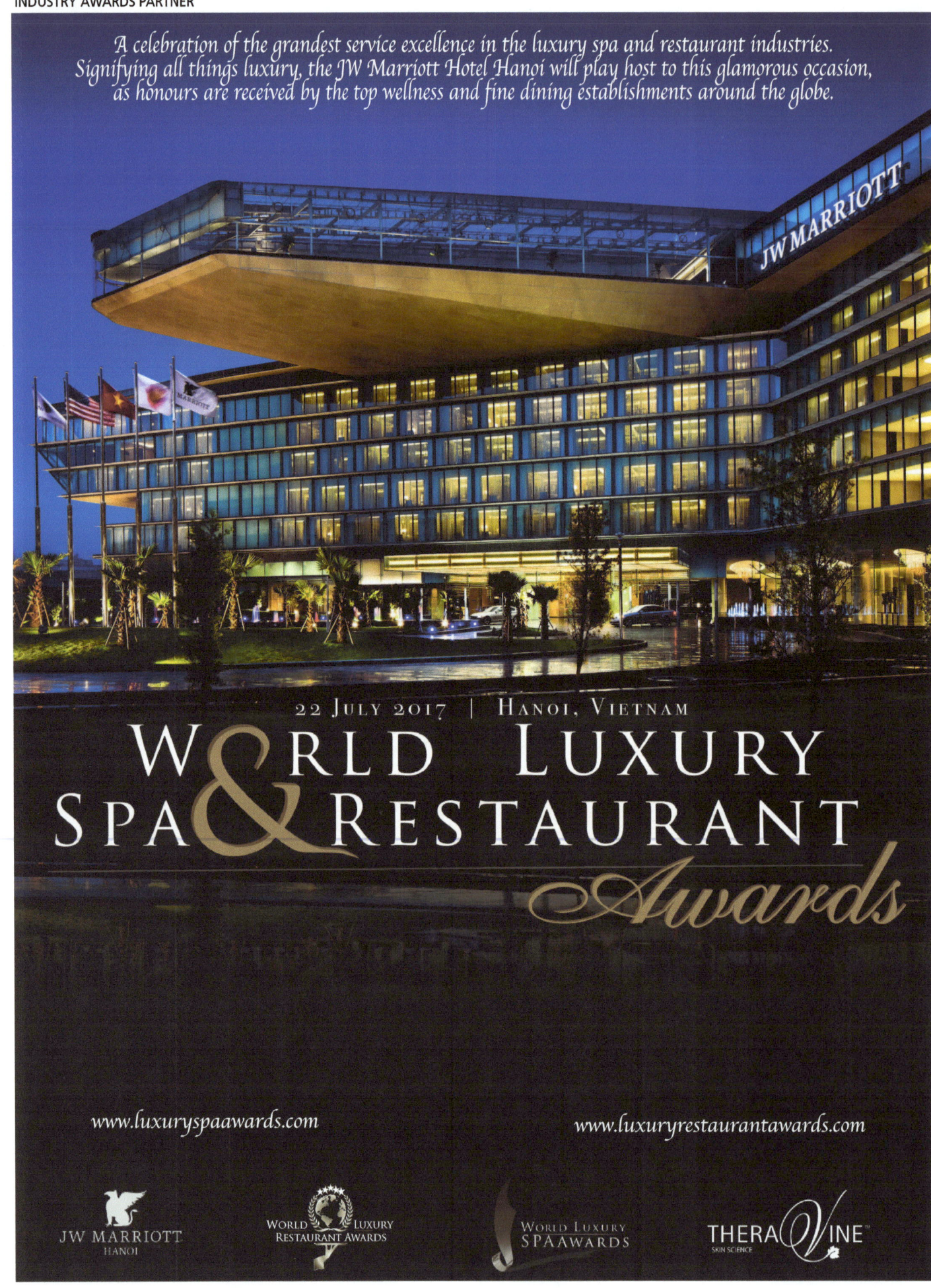

ecoplanet bamboo

A SUSTAINABLE SOLUTION FOR AFRICA

EcoPlanet Bamboo represents the first successful and the only sustainability certified commercial bamboo farms in Africa and has set the platform for certified bamboo to provide a viable tree-free, triple bottom line solution to Africa's deforestation crisis. With commercial operations in South Africa, Ghana & a smallholder expansion in East Africa underway, EcoPlanet Bamboo is leading the way for the tourism industry and others to become truly deforestation free.

EcoPlanet Bamboo has successfully restored more than 15,000 acres globally through the conversion of severely degraded land into bamboo forests that provide a suite of ecosystem services as well as the creation of more than 750 employment opportunities.

In South Africa, EcoPlanet Bamboo chose an area in the Eastern Cape where chemically heavy commercial agriculture had left soils denuded and the decline of the pineapple industry had left communities with high rates of unemployment. Since 2012 the company has owned, developed & operated the Kowie Bamboo Farm, representing South Africa's first successful commercial bamboo operation with an investment of more than US$5 million. The Kowie Bamboo Farm is the first African bamboo operation to achieve certification under the Forest Stewardship Council & has become a global showcase of landscape restoration.

EcoPlanet Bamboo is designed to provide the raw resource & an innovative manufacturing solution to industries, allowing them to switch to tree free, deforestation free products across a range of sectors. In South Africa, the bamboo farm has been developed in conjunction with onsite manufacturing by the company's subsidiary, EcoPlanet Core Carbon, with product development guided by a full R&D centre, EPB Laboratories. The bamboo from the farm is manufactured on site into a range of speciality carbonized products for water and air purification. Other applications for the sustainable tourism & hotel industry include a renewable & compostable bamboo alternative for the growing market for disposable tableware and take away food & drink packaging and with a range of side products including bamboo essential oils for cosmetics. We are proud to be launching our products through our partnership with the Mantis Collection *(see page 07)*.

The company's long term vision from its larger operations is towards the production of a clean, deforestation-free toilet paper, and luxury textiles.

18 September 2017
by
World Bamboo Organization

QUICK LINKS:

+27 (0)46 622 3540 • info@ecoplanetbamboo.com • www.ecoplanetbamboo.za.com • @EcoPlanetBambooGroup • @EcoPlanetBamboo

EcoPlanet Bamboo • ecoplanetbamboo • EcoPlanet Bamboo • EcoPlanet Bamboo

AFRICA'S SUSTAINABLE TOURISM GEMS — SPECIAL FEATURE — PARTNER

HOME SEARCH • ABOUT • GET INVOLVED • BLOG • CONTACT US | GET LISTED ON ECO ATLAS ✓

Launching Africa's sustainable tourism gems this month with a selection of South Africa's eco-friendly hotels and lodges, Tourism Tattler has partnered with Eco Atlas – an award winning eco-travel choice website. Where a featured eco-friendly property is already listed on Eco Atlas, we've shown the applicable icons.

RESOURCE USE

 **Water Saving:** 3 or more of the following practices in place: a no-leak policy, water audit, flow restrictors on taps and shower heads, dual flush toilet cisterns, harvesting rain water, utilising waste water (grey water), only watering early morning and evening, alien tree removal, planting water wise, drip irrigation system, compost toilet, garden well mulched.

 **Energy Saving:** 3 or more of the following practices in place: energy A-rated appliances, low energy bulbs, geezer blankets and/or timers, established electricity strategy such as switching off appliances and lights when not being used.

 **Recycling:** Established policy to reduce and re-use waste, the recycling of any of the following resources: Paper, Glass, Tin, Plastic and Organic Matter, on-site composting and wormeries.

 **Renewable Energy:** Utilising solar and/or wind energy through solar panels and/or wind turbines.

 **Green Design:** Incorporated into the design of the building: proper insulation, sustainable and renewable building materials, maximising light and energy from the sun, building with recycled materials, non-toxic paints and other building materials, water and energy efficiency.

 **Carbon Neutral:** Planting of trees to off-set the carbon footprint of the establishment and its guests.

EARTH FRIENDLY

 **Eco Cleaning Agents:** utilising or selling products that are fully biodegradable, free of harmful chemicals and not tested on animals.

 **Eco Body Products:** Utilising or selling body products that are fully biodegradable, free of harmful chemicals and not tested on animals.

 **Eco Packaging:** Utilising or selling fully biodegradable packaging and take-away containers made from renewable resources. Accepting returns on product packaging for re-use.

PEOPLE AND EARTH

 **Biodiversity:** no use of pesticides or poisons, planting only indigenous, conservation of indigenous flora and fauna on your property, alien vegetation removal and rehabilitation of indigenous.

 **Local Products:** utilising products grown or manufactured within a 100km radius, the producing or selling of local products.

 **Organic Food:** Utilising or selling food that is produced using a system that sustains the health of soils, ecosystems and people without the use of inputs with adverse effects for biodiversity.

 **Fair Trade:** selling products or implementing policies which contribute to sustainable development by offering better trading conditions to, and securing the rights of, marginalized producers and workers. Registered with Fair Trade Tourism or Fair Trade Label SA.

 **Empowerment:** Skills development, training and profit share programmes which empower staff and enable better working conditions and work opportunities.

ANIMAL FRIENDLY

 **Free Range Chicken:** raised in a humane manner with freedom to roam and constant access to vegetation, fresh air and fresh water. Chickens free of hormones and antibiotics (check with your supplier if they meet all these requirements)

 **Free Range Eggs:** chickens raised in a humane manner with freedom to roam and constant access to vegetation, fresh air and fresh water. Chickens free of hormones and antibiotics (check with your supplier if they meet all these requirements)

 **Badger Friendly Honey:** utilising or selling honey accredited with the Endangered Wildlife Trust certificate to ensure no honey badgers are harmed in the production of the honey.

 **Ethically Farmed Products:** utilising or selling free range meat and/or wool products that are have wildlife friendly management strategies which do not include the trapping, hunting, poisoning and killing of predators. Fair Game endorsed products.

 **Sustainable Fishing:** utilising, promoting or selling sustainable seafood from well managed fisheries as listed in the South African Sustainable Seafood Initiative (SASSI).

 **Free Range Pork:** Raised in a humane manner with freedom to roam outdoors and constant access to vegetation, fresh air and fresh water. Pigs free of hormones and antibiotics and their feed free of animal by-products (check with your supplier if they meet all these requirements)

 **Veg Or Vegan:** Serving purely vegetarian or vegan food, thereby providing healthy eating alternatives and decreasing the amount of natural resources used in the production of food.

SUSTAINABLE TOURISM SOLUTIONS   PARTNER

Join the Fair Trade Move Toward Sustainability

Fair Trade Tourism (FTT) launched a new membership programme in May aimed at tourism businesses that need support for their sustainability measures but do not have the resources to become certified in the short term.

For an annual membership fee, ranging from 1,100 (ZAR) for a sole enterprise to 6,000 (ZAR) for a business with 26-50 staff members, Fair Trade Tourism will guide businesses along the sustainability path, focusing on areas such as legal compliance, labour and staff management, reducing energy, water and waste, fair purchasing and improving market access.

Commenting on the entry level programme, Jane Edge, Managing Director of FTT said: "Our aim is to bring smaller businesses into the Fair Trade Tourism value chain, to encourage them to operate more sustainably and to expose them to tour operators who support sustainable efforts. By lowering the threshold for enterprises to access our business development services, we hope to broaden our sustainability impact and contribute to more inclusive growth of the tourism industry."

Aspirant members need to be approved by FTT's Client Advisory Committee and to sign a pledge committing them to year-on-year improvements in their sustainability measures. Applicants fill out a self-evaluation form online about their sustainability actions and FTT will produce a gap analysis highlighting areas where the business needs to improve. FTT will provide the toolkits, templates, and advice required to assist businesses along the sustainability path.

For more information, contact Thiofhi Ravele, Business Development Services Manager at thiofhi@fairtrade.travel or apply online on at www.fairtrade.travel.

Fair Trade Tourism has partnered with Tourism Tattler in supporting the aims and aspirations of the
2017 International Year of Sustainable Tourism for Development.
Through a series of editorial features published throughout this year, Tourism Tattler will be profiling a selection of
Fair Trade certified tourism businesses who meet and in many cases exceed, sustainable tourism practices.

View Fair Trade's Sustainable Tourism Gems already listed on the
UNWTO #IYSTD2017 official website at:
www.tourism4development2017.org

ACCOLADES

SPA AWARD WINNERS

Main image: **2017 Global Spa of the Year:** Harnn Heritage Spa at InterContinental Danang Sun Peninsula Resort, Vietnam.

Best Emerging Spa in Europe: AWAY Spa at the W Amsterdam, Netherlands

Best Luxury Resort Spa in Italy: GOCO Spa, Venice, Italy

Best Luxury Resort Spa in Southern Asia: Remède Spa

ACCOLADES

WORLD LUXURY SPA & RESTAURANT Awards
22 July 2017 | Hanoi, Vietnam

The World Luxury Spa Awards and **World Luxury Restaurant Awards** are established global organisations providing luxury spas and restaurants with recognition for world-class service excellence provided to guests.

Setting the basis for service industry standards around the world, the companies pride themselves on acknowledging luxury spas and restaurants in their relevant categories during the annual voting phase.

Votes are garnered through various marketing channels from guests, showcasing yet again the true value of service excellence.

Voting for the 2017 award year saw over 100,000 votes from happy customers around the globe placing their stamp of approval on their establishment of choice.

"One of the most favourable ways to award service excellence is by allowing people to have their say, and hearing from the public is a popular manner in which to make a decision on where you will stay, spa or dine. An award of this stature signifies quality, service delivery and much sought after luxury. All of which have made our participants what they are today, winners in the luxury hospitality field." says Marna Lourens, Executive Manager for the World Luxury Spa Awards.

Winning participants receive awards in their respective categories on a country, regional, continent and global basis, purely from guest votes.

The 2017 grand gala celebration, the night which honours these fine establishments, took place on 22 July and was proudly hosted by the exquisite JW Marriott Hotel Hanoi. Nearly 200 participants joined the evening in anticipation of what was to come.

Host venue for the 2017 World Luxury Spa and Restaurant Awards gala celebrations, JW Marriott Hotel, Hanoi, Vietnam.

▼ Continued on page 14

The St. Regis Bali Resort, Indonesia

Best Luxury Medical Spa in Asia: **The Farm** at San Benito, Philippines

For more information about the vi

ACCOLADES

RESTAURANT AWARD WINNERS

Best Luxury Haute Cuisine: **Carnival by Tresind**, United Arab Emirates.

Best Luxury Chinese Cuisine: **China Blue** by Jereme Leung, Philippines.

Best Luxury Hotel Restaurant in Africa:

Main image: **2017 Global Restaurant of the Year: Ithaa Undersea Restaurant**, Rangali Island, Maldives.

ACCOLADES

22 JULY 2017 | HANOI, VIETNAM
World Luxury Spa & Restaurant Awards

La Table, Royal Mansour, Morocco.

Best Luxury Unique Experience in Europe: **SnowRestaurant**, Kemi, Finland

"The most coveted award on the evening is our Global Spa and Global Restaurant of the Year Awards. Each year the task to determine these top establishments begins after voting has closed and we announce to our winners if they have been successful. We are six senior managers who take weeks to decide, as voting is not the only criteria we look at to bestow this prestigious award. A multitude of factors come in to play; brand, location, overall guest satisfaction from online reviews, services and facilities, design, and even menu offerings whether spa or restaurant.

"It is important to look at each establishment as an individual as well, some are on an island, some are in cities or in a desert, it is not always possible to compare apples with apples when defining luxury. This year the focus was on unique design with a touch of classy elegance, and we were as such proud to award Global Spa of the Year to Harnn Heritage Spa at InterContinental Danang Sun Peninsula Resort, and Global Restaurant of the Year to Ithaa Undersea Restaurant at Conrad Maldives Rangali Island," says Joanna Evans, Marketing Communications Manager for the World Luxury Awards.

The evening was as glamorous as one would expect from a JW Marriott brand hotel; a delectable 6-course fine dining menu paired with fine wines and champagne from Moët et Chandon. Entertainment included a Dragon Dance, a Vietnamese based string quartet performance by Độc Câm - Toxic Quartet, and a local Ao Dai Dance, all of which added to the evening's Asian flair.

"We welcome luxury establishments from around the globe to participate in these exciting awards, to proudly show the world what they have to offer in terms of luxury and service excellence." says Linda Cooper, Executive Manager for the World Luxury Restaurant Awards.

Tourism Tattler congratulates all 2017 World Luxury Spa and Restaurant Award winners. In particular, we pay tribute to the following Africa based winners who have excelled on the global spa and restaurant stage:

Global Winners (Africa):

Spas: South Africa: AM Spa - Hoedspruit for best Luxury Safari Spa; Gatsby Spa for best Luxury Spa Group; Indigo Fields for best Luxury Countryside Spa; Langaro Lifestyle Centre for Best Spa Manager.

Restaurants: Kenya: Talisman Restaurant for best Eclectic (International) Cuisine; Morocco: Nür Restaurant for best Moroccan Cuisine; South Africa: Karibu for best South African Cuisine.

In total, Africa based spas and restaurants took home 78 wins across the continent!

A full list of all 2017 spa winners can be viewed HERE *and restaurant winners* HERE.

Tourism Tattler is proud to have been associated with the 2017 World Luxury Spa and Restaurant Awards as a media partner and look forward to featuring the forthcoming 2017 World Luxury Hotel Awards.

For more information about the World Luxury Restaurant Awards visit: www.luxuryrestaurantawards.com.

BUSINESS & FINANCE

Market Intelligence Report

SATSA – Southern Africa Tourism Services Association | Grant Thornton

The information below was extracted from data available as at **04 August 2017**. By Martin Jansen van Vuuren of Grant Thornton.

ARRIVALS

The latest available data from Statistics South Africa is for **January to May 2017***:

	Current period	Change over same period last year
UK	209 891	2.5%
Germany	153 232	14.8%
USA	142 847	8.2%
India	42 968	2.8%
China (incl Hong Kong)	43 260	-13.3%
Overseas Arrivals	1 144 088	10.6%
African Arrivals	3 159 394	-2.4%
Total Foreign Arrivals	4 308 358	0.7%

HOTEL STATS

The latest available data from STR Global is for **January to May 2017**:

Current period	Average Room Occupancy (ARO)	Average Room Rate (ARR)	Revenue Per Available Room (RevPAR)
All Hotels in SA	64.2%	R 1 269	R 815
All 5-star hotels in SA	66.8%	R 2 360	R 1 576
All 4-star hotels in SA	65.7%	R 1 172	R 771
All 3-star hotels in SA	63.3%	R 946	R 599
Change over same period last year			
All Hotels in SA	-0.8%	5.9%	5.1%
All 5-star hotels in SA	-1.3%	6.0%	4.7%
All 4-star hotels in SA	1.2%	6.2%	7.5%
All 3-star hotels in SA	0.2%	3.3%	3.5%

ACSA DATA

The latest available data from ACSA is for **January to June 2017**:

Change over same period last year	Passengers arriving on International Flights	Passengers arriving on Regional Flights	Passengers arriving on Domestic Flights
OR Tambo International	3.9%	-1.6%	0.6%
Cape Town International	26.1%	3.0%	2.9%
King Shaka International	10.4%	N/A	6.2%

CAR RENTAL DATA

The latest available data from SAVRALA is for **January to December 2016**:

	Current period	Change over same period last year
Industry Rental Days	16 936 276	7%
Industry Utilisation	71.6%	1.5%
Industry Revenue	5 294 680 207	12%

WHAT THIS MEANS FOR MY BUSINESS

Tourism enterprises should note the nuances that the data highlights with regard to source markets and regional spread. Overseas tourists continue to grow with strong growth from the German and USA market but subdued growth from the UK and Indian market. Passengers arriving on International Flights are growing strongly to Cape Town and King Shaka but is more subdued to OR Tambo. Tourism enterprises specialising in the German and USA market to Cape Town would be doing well, while enterprises specialising in the UK and Indian market to Gauteng would need to increase their business development activities.

*Note that African Arrivals plus Overseas Arrivals do not add to Total Foreign Arrivals due to the exclusion of unspecified arrivals, which could not be allocated to either African or Overseas.

For more information contact Martin at Grant Thornton on +27 (0)21 417 8838 or visit: http://www.gt.co.za

BUSINESS & FINANCE

GLOBAL Tourism Statistics

Strong results in the first part of 2017

International tourist arrivals worldwide grew by 6% in January-April of 2017 compared to the same period last year, with business confidence reaching its highest levels in a decade. Sustained growth in most major destinations and a steady rebound in others drove results. Prospects for May-August 2017 remain high.

Destinations worldwide received 369 million international tourists (overnight visitors) in the first four months of the year, 21 million more than in the same months of 2016 (+6%), according to the latest UNWTO World Tourism Barometer. The January-April period usually represents some 28% of the yearly total and covers the winter season of the Northern Hemisphere and the summer season of the Southern Hemisphere, as well as the Chinese New Year and Easter holidays, among others.

International arrivals reported by destinations around the world were positive overall, with very few exceptions. Most of 2016's strong performers maintained momentum, while destinations that struggled in previous years continued to rebound in the first part of 2017. This is especially reflected in the better results of the Middle East (+10%), Africa (+8%) and Europe (+6%). Asia and the Pacific (6%) and the Americas (+4%) continued to enjoy robust growth.

"Destinations that were affected by negative events during 2016 are showing clear signs of recovery in a very short period of time, and this is very welcoming news for all, but particularly for those whose livelihoods depend on tourism in these destinations," said UNWTO Secretary-General Taleb Rifai.

"As we celebrate 2017 as the International Year of Sustainable Tourism for Development, we welcome the continued development of tourism and recall that with growth comes increased responsibility to ensure tourism can contribute to sustainability in all its three pillars – economic, social and environmental. Growth is never the enemy and it is our responsibility to manage it in a sustainable manner," he added.

Regional Results

International arrivals in Europe (+6%) rebounded in January-April after mixed results last year, as confidence returned to some destinations that were impacted by security incidents, while others continued to grow strongly. Results improved particularly in Southern Mediterranean Europe (+9% as compared to +1% in 2016) and Western Europe (+4% as opposed to +0% in 2016). Northern Europe (+9%) continued to record strong growth, while Central and Eastern Europe recorded 4% more international arrivals, in line with results of last year.

In Asia and the Pacific, international arrivals were up 6% through April with sound results across all four subregions. South Asia (+14%) led growth, followed by Oceania (+7%), South-East Asia (+6%) and North-East Asia (+5%).

International arrivals in the Americas were up 4% with strong results in South America and Central America (both +7%), while arrivals in North America grew by 3% and in the Caribbean by 2%.

Limited data available for Africa points to an 8% increase in international arrivals, with North Africa (+18%) recovering strongly. International arrivals in the Middle East rebounded by an estimated 10% following a 4% decline in 2016.

Positive prospects for May-August

The current strong momentum is reflected in the UNWTO Panel of Tourism Experts confidence index, based on evaluations and prospects of worldwide experts surveyed every four months since 2003. Experts evaluated tourism performance in the first four months of 2017 with the highest score in 12 years, clearly exceeding their already positive expectations from the start of the period. Responses to the survey were strongest from Europe, in line with the rebound in arrivals.

Experts also show strong confidence in the current May-August period, as their prospects are the most optimistic in a decade, also driven by upbeat expectations in Europe. The May-August period includes the peak tourism season in most of the world's major tourism destinations and source markets.

Useful links:

UNWTO World Tourism Barometer
UNWTO Tourism Highlights, 2016 Edition
Infographics

BUSINESS & FINANCE

Economic Benefits of Hosting Events in AFRICA

An Independent report has revealed a seven-figure economic boost to destinations that have hosted the Africa Hotel Investment Forum over a six year period.

By **Martin Jansen van Vuuren**.

The significant economic benefits to host countries of the influential Africa Hotel Investment Forum (AHIF) have been quantified in an independent assessment by the international audit, tax and advisory experts, Grant Thornton. The total contribution to African economies is estimated at $16.8 million and since inception, it is estimated that AHIF has been responsible for deals cumulatively worth over $4billion.

The headline figures include direct, indirect and induced financial benefits – accepted economic multipliers – and run from the first AHIF in Morocco in 2011 to Rwanda last year.

On average, hosting an AHIF event brings a million dollars in direct benefit to the local economy, an additional 1.4 million dollars in indirect benefit and a substantial six-figure sum in tax to the host government.

Evidence of the successful impact of AHIF – organised by Bench Events – comes ahead of the seventh edition taking place in Kigali, from 10 to 12 October and, like last year, running alongside the airline route development conference, AviaDev, which together attract some of the leading executives from the worlds of aviation and hotels, with top government officials and ministers.

AHIF's benefits: Key findings – over 6 years:
- Direct contribution of AHIF to local economies projected at $6.9 million.
- Additional $9.9 million generated through indirect and induced impact, ie boosting local suppliers, increasing local spending power.
- Projected total of $1.1 million paid in taxes in various host countries.
- A projected total of 5,462 jobs – temporary or permanent – created or sustained.
- Delegate survey indicates a total deal value of $124 million, an average of $4.6 million per deal – translated for all AHIF events between 2011 and 2016, deals total an estimated $4.4 billion.

A breakdown of AHIF's economic impact can be accessed here.

One key gauge of AHIF's success is the high-level of the delegates it attracts – the attending CEO's and MD's do not only spend more than average by staying in the best hotels but much more importantly, they are people with the ability to make decisions, including whether or not to invest in a destination – and that's reflected in the value of deals done.

The report also highlights the fact that host economies benefit from wide media coverage and from the credential of hosting a top-level conference like AHIF. Doing so helps to attract further events, which boost local companies and provide job opportunities as well as the chance to develop skills.

Regarding Africa's broader economic prospects, the growth of African countries may have slowed at present because of commodity prices, but commodity prices will rise again, and given hotel development lead-in times, which are three years on average, and taking into account the life of the asset, which is decades after the hotel is built, this is a good moment for investment, in my view.

And my view is supported by Jonathan Worsley, chairman of Bench events, who says: "We are gratified that this report bears out what we've always believed: that hosting AHIF adds value to the places we visit and the conference is a great place to discuss deals which benefit tourism in Africa. This year's event will be our most comprehensive and exciting with an outstanding line-up of speakers, first-hand advice from experts and unique networking opportunities. Rwanda is a prime example of what can be achieved in our sector by a country that is determined to use tourism to propel itself forward and we're pleased to be back again in October."

For more information visit www.Africa-Conference.com

About the author: Martin Jansen van Vuuren *holds the post of Strategic Development & Planning Director at* Grant Thornton *Cape.*

BUSINESS & FINANCE

Business Tourism in AFRICA Continues to Expand

Perceptions of Africa as a business destination have changed vastly in recent times. The ICCA 2016 rankings reveal that Africa is growing in popularity as a destination for business tourism.

By **Zandre Campos**.

It has been perceived that doing business or hosting events in Africa can be complicated. However, there has been a recent boom in both conferences and large sporting events, which has improved business tourism significantly. While Africa is not as popular as other countries, like the UAE or the UK, they do have top-notch venues and spectacular stays for visitors. Countries throughout Africa offer a surplus of opportunities to host business conferences and tourism has become a crucial component of Africa's economy.

The International Convention Association (ICCA) recently announced the 2016 rankings for international business meetings and many African countries were included on the list. The ICCA in Africa has about 39 member organizations in over 9 countries and over the past few years, Africa's rankings have improved. According to the latest ICCA ranking of Africa, South Africa, Morocco and Rwanda are the highest ranked meeting, incentive, conference and event (MICE) destinations in Africa. In addition, the highest ranked cities are Cape Town, Marrakesh, and Kigali.

With magnificent sites and views, South Africa, specifically the city of Cape Town, has had great success with business tourism. Currently, Cape Town is ranked in the top 40 destinations for business tourism in the world and has gone up 15 places on that ranking in a short amount of time. There have been about 62 meetings in Cape Town relating to a variety of topics such as education, technology, and medical sciences and it is predicted to grow even more in the future.

The country of Morocco has had a significant increase of business tourism and is ranked the second highest by the ICCA. Recently, the city of Marrakesh was named one of the most popular travel destinations in the world, according to Trip Advisor because of its charming culture and welcoming hospitality. According to the ICCA ranking of 2016, there were 37 meetings in Morocco and 19 in the city of Marrakesh. With new ideas and strategies to increase tourism, Morocco hopes to increase business tourism through the promotion of the country's culture, locations, and sustainability even more than before.

With its current third place ranking, Rwanda has improved its ranking significantly since 2014, when it ranked 13th. With the recent addition of 5-star hotels, including the Radisson Blu and Marriott Kigali, business tourism has skyrocketed. Additionally, the English and French speaking country of Rwanda is ranked the ninth safest country globally for tourists. The capital city of Kigali was ranked third and it is the location of the first Marriot Hotel in Sub-Saharan Africa. Marriot Kigali consists of 254 rooms and 10 conference halls, contributing to the increase in space for conferences. In addition, a recent report from the World Economic Forum shows that Rwanda's international tourist arrivals are at 987,000 and international tourism inbound receipts are at $317.8 million.

There are many other countries with distinct cultures and experiences that are also tourism-ready economies to host business conferences. Additionally, languages that are spoken in each country will help determine the best fit for businesses. Conventions headquartered in the UK will most likely go to English speaking countries in Africa including South Africa, Namibia, Kenya, Nigeria, and Rwanda. Events from France would typically go to the French speaking countries of the Republic of the Congo, the Ivory Coast and Rwanda. Those from Portugal will go to countries where Portuguese is spoken, such as Angola, Mozambique and Cape Verde.

By looking at ICCA's recent rankings and the overall improvements of countries in Africa, it is evident that Africa is a great place to host business conferences. Africa has the potential to be one of the most popular destinations for business tourism and will continue to improve on their ranking.

About the author: *Zandre Campos* is chairman and CEO of ABO Capital, an international investment firm that invests in companies in the healthcare, energy, transportation, hospitality, technology and real estate sectors throughout Africa.

DESTINATIONS

Discover Luxury in
KENYA

Kenya is an exceptional African destination for luxury safari and beach holidays with variety to suit different segments; couples, honeymooners or families.

Kenya is renown as the world's leading safari destination and indeed in many ways, Kenya is the ultimate African destination. Luxury travel in Kenya provides travellers with an intimate window into the heart of Africa.

Located near the equator, it offers savannahs teeming with game, cultures as old as time and unchanged by the modern world, forests, snow-capped peaks, deserts, beaches and even coral reefs.

The entire spectrum of luxury hotels, tented camps, endless opportunity for adventure and breathtaking moments of discovery wrapped in the warmth of the people is what makes Kenya's safaris so luxurious. The next time you book your flight for this type of unforgettable experience, you will be spoilt for choice.

Beach & Golf Safari

Imagine having a round of golf in the morning, and in the same afternoon, basking on one of Kenya's pristine white sandy beaches.

Alternatively, you can have a round of golf in the morning, followed by a ride in a glass bottom boat, to marvel at nature in one of the richest marine parks you will ever see.

Kenya offers you tropical sunshine, blue skies and endless silver-white beaches backed by waving palms and tranquil lagoons. For aquatic mammal lover's, you can take things up a notch and embrace a personal encounter with dolphins.

DESTINATIONS

Hot Air Balloon Safari

For honeymooners, leisure seekers, couple's wishing to enjoy their excursion in Kenya; perhaps this is a great opportunity to exchange vows while aboard a balloon safari in Maasai Mara – one of the world's famous National Game Reserves.

The balloon safari allows you to traverse the vast Savannah, have a perfect view of the big-five, and catch a view of the new 8th wonder of the world that is the wildebeest migration among other different species of wildlife.

After the excitement of a Balloon safari, one would require a relaxed evening and Kenya's many luxurious safari lodges and tented camps offer the required tranquillity.

Unrivalled Exclusivity

Looking to enjoy exclusive relaxation away from the multitudes? Travel to any of Kenya's luxury five-star lodges. Movement between lodges is not a challenge thanks to superb connectivity, witnessed by the numerous airstrips that enable domestic flights to shuttle tourists within a short period.

The unrivalled exclusivity of Kenya's lodges allows you to indulge in the pleasures of any given moment, making for a unique and tailored Kenyan experience.

Be accorded specialised attention to meet your every expectation, be it dining in the wild as you watch the sun set over the Savannah or just lying basking in the sun in front of your very own private pool looking over the picturesque views.

DESTINATIONS

Spa & Wellness Safari

With the anticipation of a relaxing beach holiday and many photo-snapping game safari moments, Kenya has thrown in an equally exciting recipe to the holiday menu, which guarantees total relaxation while simultaneously invigorating the mind, body and soul.

Kenya's four- and five-star hotels, lodges and beach resorts boast well-equipped spas staffed by highly trained therapists.

Having a spa treatment, be it a simple massage or a hot stone massage that sinks deeper into muscle tissues, one is sure to uncover the true meaning of bliss.

Visit any of Kenya's hotels, lodges, camps and other accommodation spa facilities to begin this invigorating experience.

Culinary Experience

Beyond the adrenalin filled adventure, Kenya also offers varied delicacies that mirror unique lifestyle and ethnic groups within the country.

From backpackers to newlyweds in a quaint restaurant, and the families in five-star hotels, a sumptuous culinary experience awaits you all.

Discover the magic of Kenya at www.magicalkenya.com

DESTINATIONS

South Africa's Ultimate Journey

Route Map of 100 Worthy Places

In collaboration with MotorHappy, an Imperial Group subsidiary, and with New Zealand travel writer Jen Miller of JenReviews.com, here's Tourism Tattler's route of 100 worthy places for an ultimate journey. The #UltimateJourneySA campaign and competition aims to create South Africa's Ultimate Road Trip based on the amount of votes a location receives throughout the campaign, which ends in August. Anyone who adds or votes for a location will be in the draw to win a road trip for up to four people, valued at R50 000!

NORTHERN CAPE

001 The Big Hole (Kimberley)

The Kimberley Big Hole is an interesting tour if you're interested in diamonds. The De Beer family has been mining for 120 years and the mine at Kimberley managed to yield 2722 Kilograms of diamonds. You will also be able to see homes and churches built in the 1800's that have been preserved. There is a lot of history in Kimberly, including the flawless 70 carat champagne coloured Kimberley diamond, which was set in the Russian Crown Jewels but eventually sold to a private buyer.

Vote for this location on **South Africa's Ultimate Journey** HERE.

002 Kgalagadi Transfrontier Park (Upington)

Soaring temperatures that rise to 40'c, red sand dunes and stars that fill the night sky, the Kgalagadi desert is a magical African experience. You will be able to see many many animals in their natural habitat. Hear the roar of lions at night or the haunting laugh of a hyena. This is a magical experience not to be missed.

Vote for this location on **South Africa's Ultimate Journey** HERE.

003 Augrabies Waterfall (Augrabies)

This 56-meter waterfall is set in an arid and rocky part of South Africa, so it seems out of place in this desolate part of the country. The Augrabies Falls National Park is a beautiful place to visit, with many hikes, and interesting rock formations to see.

Vote for this location HERE.

004 Orange River Rafting (Vioolsdrif)

Something for the adventurous! River rafting down the Orange River is an exciting and different way to see South Africa. The rapids range from easy to moderate. The tour offers half day to 6-day trips. The 6-day trip will be about 65 to 120km. Each night you will stop on the river bank, camp and enjoy a lovely meal.

Vote for this location on **South Africa's Ultimate Journey** HERE.

005 Namaqua National Park (Springbok)

Velvet black skies twinkle with stars at night, while down below the ground is covered with millions of daisies as far as the eye can see. The Namaqua National Park is a place of contrast; with a dry arid type desert, to beautiful oceans and then the most exquisite part, the Namaqua daisies.

Vote for this location on **South Africa's Ultimate Journey** HERE.

WESTERN CAPE

006 Riebeek Kasteel (Cape Town)

Nestled in the Kasteel Mountains is the little town of Riebeek Kasteel surrounded by vineyards, olive groves, and unforgettable mountains. Riebeek Kasteel has been called the Mediterranean of Africa. This is a magical little town is one of the oldest in South Africa.

Vote for this location on **South Africa's Ultimate Journey** HERE.

DESTINATIONS

007 Robben Island *(Cape Town)*

Robben Island provides a historical and informative tour that reflects the social injustice of Apartheid. It's located 6.9 km out to sea from the beautiful Bloubergstrand suburb of Cape Town. The island had been used for the imprisonment of criminals. You will be able to go on tours of the foreboding prisons. Nelson Mandela was imprisoned on Robben Island for 18 years and eventually became a true inspiration for all South Africans and people around the world.

Vote for this location on **South Africa's Ultimate Journey HERE**.

008 Table Mountain *(Cape Town)*

This massive Table Mountain has incredible views over Cape Town and is a must see attraction in South Africa! You can either take a short 2-hour hike up Table Mountain or enjoy a cable car ride up to the top. The views from the top are magnificent!

Vote for this location on **South Africa's Ultimate Journey HERE**.

009 V&A Waterfront *(Cape Town)*

The V&A Waterfront is a wonderful stop for good food, great shopping, and awesome live music. There are more than 450 stores to enjoy.
Vote for this location on **South Africa's Ultimate Journey HERE**.

010 The Old Biscuit Mill *(Cape Town)*

This adorable warm and quaint little village in Woodstock is for those who love good food, awesome music, and a trendy vibe. The Old Biscuit Mill is filled with artists, photographers, architects and food connoisseurs. The village actually used to be a biscuit mill and is filled with history too.

Vote for this location on **South Africa's Ultimate Journey HERE**.

011 District 6 Museum *(Cape Town)*

District six was a suburb during the Apartheid years that had as many as 1900 families living there. The families were forcibly removed from their homes so that the area could become a "whites only" neighbourhood. 60 000 people were relocated to the Cape Flats. This was a gross injustice and at the District Six museum, you will be able to learn more about this bleak part in South Africa's history..

Vote for this location on **South Africa's Ultimate Journey HERE**.

Looking at the route map at the top of this page, we start our 9 province Ultimate Journey in the Northern Cape and drive an (almost) circular route through the Western Cape, Eastern Cape, Freestate, KwaZulu-Natal, Mpumalanga, Limpopo, North West and end in Gauteng. View the remaining 89 worthy places of our route selection on our website under the Destination News tab.

EVENTS

NEWS, VIEWS, AND REVIEWS FOR THE TRAVEL TRADE IN, TO AND OUT OF AFRICA

Proud Media Partner to THINC Africa 2017

Bringing Africa to the World & the World to Africa

www.tourismtattler.com

EVENTS

THINC Africa Launches Business Meetings
30-31 Aug 2017 Cape Town

Delegates registered to attend the Tourism, Hotel Investment and Networking Conference (THINC) Africa event this year, can now schedule appointments to meet with speakers and fellow delegates to discuss business deals. The conference is taking place at the FNB Portside Building in Cape Town's iconic V&A Waterfront precinct.

By Des Langkilde.

Business meetings and deal making

Adding to THINC Africa's reputation as being THE event to attend in this part of the globe, the addition of a Matchmaking and Meeting Service for registered delegates to conduct business deals during the event is a first for the conference industry in Africa.

This year's event is expecting 200 delegates, up from last year's 160, thus providing ample opportunity to network with peers and business contacts, allowing delegates to discover new and exciting opportunities in this fast expanding market.

Pitch & Match

By partnering with Pitch and Match – a business matchmaking application for live and online events *(read more on page 28)* – THINC Africa enables registered delegates to conduct business deals during the event. To ensure that the time that delegates invest is worthwhile, registrants can profile, match, interact, and pre-schedule meetings.

One-on-one meetings with speakers and delegates can be arranged at a location and time to fit between slots in the conference programme and manage these in one simple user-friendly environment. Email alerts for meeting requests can also be received.

New delegates will receive their login access details for Pitch and Match within 1 working day of registering for THINC Africa 2017.

Meet top hoteliers and investors

Now you can schedule meetings and conduct business deals with top hotelier and hospitality experts, including developers and both debt and equity funders, such as Stephen Claassen (Provincial Head, FNB), Adrian Gardiner (Chairman, Mantis Collection); Tim Smith (Managing Director, HVS Cape Town), Sisa Ngebulana (CEO of Rebosis and Billion Group), Mike Collini (VP Development SSA, Hilton Group), Roeland Vos (CEO, Belmond), Dimitris Manikis (VP Business Development, RCI), and a lot more. *Click* here *for a list.*

Investment opportunities

During the conference sessions, you can discover investment opportunities and options in various territories on the African Continent (including Mauritius, Seychelles and Mozambique) and meet the people who can facilitate these deals.

Recognition

The inaugural THINC Africa Awards are open to nominees throughout Africa to honour hotels, general managers and students. *Click* here *to nominate or enter the awards.*

Networking

In addition to pre-scheduled meetings, a cocktail party at Cape Town's iconic Belmond Mount Nelson Hotel provides an opportunity to network with delegates and speakers.

"THINC Africa provides a perfect platform to engage with hotel brands, investors, and management companies, real estate developers, bankers, and fund representatives as well as public and private hotel, tourism and convention agencies," says Tim Smith, Managing Director of HVS Cape Town.

For more information visit www.thincafrica.hvsconferences.com

EVENTS

Enabling DEAL MAKING at Live & Online TRAVEL TRADE EVENTS

To increase the economic impact of events and create a win-win situation for destinations and business tourists, the Meetings, Incentive, Conference and Events (MICE) industry in Africa needs effective technology to support business deals. Pitch and Match – a business matchmaking app for live and online events – provides a perfect solution.

By **Des Langkilde**.

Using the latest Africa Hotel Investment Forum's delegate deal values as a yard stick, their independent report of $124 million – an average of $4.6 million per deal and $4.4 billion for all AHIF events over 5 years – serves as testimony to the value of deal-making at events *(see page 18)*. And with Africa's international tourism growth expected to rise by 8% for the remainder of 2017 *(see page 17)*, the potential for business deal making at live and online events has never been better as business tourism in Africa continues to expand.

Technology ranging from simple apps to comprehensive meeting planners at event websites have become a mainstay of exhibitions and conferences around the world.

However, according to Robert Bol, CEO of Pitch and Match – a business matchmaking application for live and online events – event technology must extend far beyond the day of an event by providing year-round support for event organisers. To discover how his company's technology compliments deal making, Tourism Tattler (t) interviewed Robert Bol (**RB**).

t: How do Pitch and Match enable deal making?

RB: Pitch and Match connects delegates with speakers, exhibitors and each other by delivering the content they need and the connections they value. To ensure that the time visitors invest at events is worthwhile, the participant can profile, match, interact, pre-schedule meetings and conference sessions. It all ends up in their personal event schedule.

Participants can arrange one-on-one meetings either at specific on-site or off-site locations during the event or conduct online video meetings. It only takes one click to start a high-quality video call. There's no disconnect. The participant stays in the browser.

The event organiser decides how each participant can engage and use their personal event schedule. Before participants get access the organiser automatically grants (or sells) each group specific privileges and limitations.

t: What feedback have you had from users?

RB: Our customers have told us that Pitch and Match has become a fundamental part of their event experience and that matchmaking and the ability to make deals are the key reasons for participants to register for their events.

t: What sets Pitch and Match apart from the competition?

RB: Pitch and Match is the first business matchmaking app in the world to integrate a video call feature directly into the app itself.

t: Is the technology easy to use?

RB: As a browser app, Pitch and Match can run on a desktop or tablet and participants can also check out their event schedule on their smartphone.

From an event organisers perspective, they can set-up Pitch and Match in less than 30 minutes. They can also use our Wordpress plugin and API to integrate seamlessly into their existing online community, event website and registration flow.

t: Is online business match making a threat to live events?

RB: Online events are here to stay and, rather than being a threat, event organisers can actually benefit from it.

People attend online business events because it enables them to reach out to the world in less time, and at la ower cost. To grow their business year round, many destination managers and event organisers have already embraced online events. In doing so, they have been able to reach new audiences and maintain strong relationships with existing ones. They've increased their global reach because there's no restriction on attendees when it comes to online events, and location doesn't matter. Online events also help organisers generate extra income year round.

t: Can you give us examples of Pitch and Match's application at events?

RB: This year alone, Pitch and Match has facilitated 300 events with 150,000 attendees in more than 50 countries. The Belize Virtual Expo won an Award for the Belize Tourism Board. They used Pitch and Match to enable the destination managers from Belize to conduct business in pre-scheduled video calls with travel agents, tour operators and others. Readers can discover how this works by watching our YouTube video.

Our Service Partner in Latin America decided to build the Online Latin America Travel Trade Community, which has become the place to sign up for live and online events.

t: What about Africa based events?

RB: Pitch and Match are proud to have appointed Tourism Tattler as our Service Partner in Africa, and look forward to enabling the first live deal making event in Africa at the HVS THINC Africa Conference in Cape Town, South Africa this August *(see page 27)*.

For more information visit www.pitchandmatch.com

EVENTS

Zimbabwe's *Premium* Travel Expo

Organised by Zimbabwe Tourism, the 2017 edition of the annual Sanganai/Hlanganani World Tourism Expo will showcase the widest variety of Africa's best tourism products to international visitors and media from across the world.

The Sanganai/Hlanganani World Tourism Expo (SHWTE) is the successor of Shanyai/Vakatshani, the Zimbabwe International Travel Expo (ZITE) that was held annually at the Harare International Conference Centre. ZITE started as a small expo in 1982 and grew over the years to become one of Africa's leading tourism showcases by 2007.

The past nine editions of the SHWTE were a resounding success and attracted leading African destinations and major world tourism markets such as South Africa, Botswana, Malaysia, China, Zambia, Malawi, Kenya, Mozambique, Namibia, Indonesia, India, Italy and many others. The editions have seen the whole world converging in Zimbabwe in the form of high calibre international buyers as well as exhibitors.

The 2017 edition will be held in the country's second largest city, Bulawayo, and is expected to ride on the successes gained by the previous editions and is an opportunity not to be missed.

The Expo targets among other exhibitors the following:
- National Tourism Boards
- Embassies
- International Airlines
- Tourism destinations
- Leading Tour Wholesalers, Tour Operators, and Travel Agents
- Leading Hotel Chains of the world
- Car Hire and Transport Operators
- Suppliers of goods and services to the tourism industry
- Investors
- Government Ministries
- Parastatals

DATES AND TIMES:

SHWTE 2017 will run for five days starting on Wednesday 27 September and ending on Sunday 01 October. The event is closed to the public in trade days but opens to the public on the last day:
- 27 - 30 September trade days
- 01 October public day.

Opening times are:
- 0900 – 1700 hrs

THE HOST COUNTRY

Zimbabwe – *A World of Wonders*

Zimbabwe is a wonderful, friendly and welcoming destination, situated on a high plateau in Southern Africa and lies between the Zambezi and the Limpopo rivers. such as its Wonderful People and Culture, Rich History and heritage, the Great Zimbabwe – the grand Medieval Palace, the Majestic Victoria Falls – Mosi-oa-Tunya, Pristine Wildlife and Nature, the Mystique of the Eastern Highlands and the Mythical Lake Kariba & the Mighty Zambezi. It is a landlocked country, bordered by Zambia, Mozambique, South Africa and Botswana. The climate is generally warm, with a daily sunshine average of seven hours all year round. Zimbabwe is a plural society where people of different races live in harmony. Zimbabweans living in urban areas have a westernized lifestyle, while in the country areas many African traditions have been preserved.

THE HOST CITY

Bulawayo – *The City of Kings*

Bulawayo – candidly known as the "City of Kings" – is the host city for the 2017 Sanganai/Hlanganani World Tourism Expo. The city is rich in culture and history and is a must visit for anyone touring Zimbabwe. Bulawayo was the home of King Lobengula. It is located within easy reach of Hwange National Park, The Victoria Falls (one of the wonders of the world), The Matobo Hills where Cecil John Rhodes and King Mzilikazi are buried. Also situated near Bulawayo are the two UNESCO World Heritage Sites of Matobo National Park and the Khame Ruins.

THE VENUE

Zimbabwe International Exhibition Centre (ZIEC).

Situated within the city of Bulawayo, the Zimbabwe International Exhibition (ZIEC) also known as the Zimbabwe International Trade Fair Grounds Centre has excellent facilities and is easily accessible from all areas of the city. ZIEC plays host to some of the leading international exhibitions such as the Zimbabwe International Trade Fair (ZITF), Mine Entra and many others.

THE BENEFITS

Benefits Of Attending #Sanganai2017

Meet and network with (Sanganai/Hlanganani) exhibitors, visiting buyers, investors, and suppliers of services to the tourism sector from all over the world.
- Establish strategic business partnerships with world tourism players
- Showcase your destination, products, and services
- Acquire knowledge about different source markets
- Derive value from well structured, themed and informative International tourism conferences and workshops
- Interact with Travel Media from all corners of the world
- Establish strategic partnerships with other destinations/Cities,
- Network across Ministerial divides.

For more information visit www.sanganaitourismexpo.com

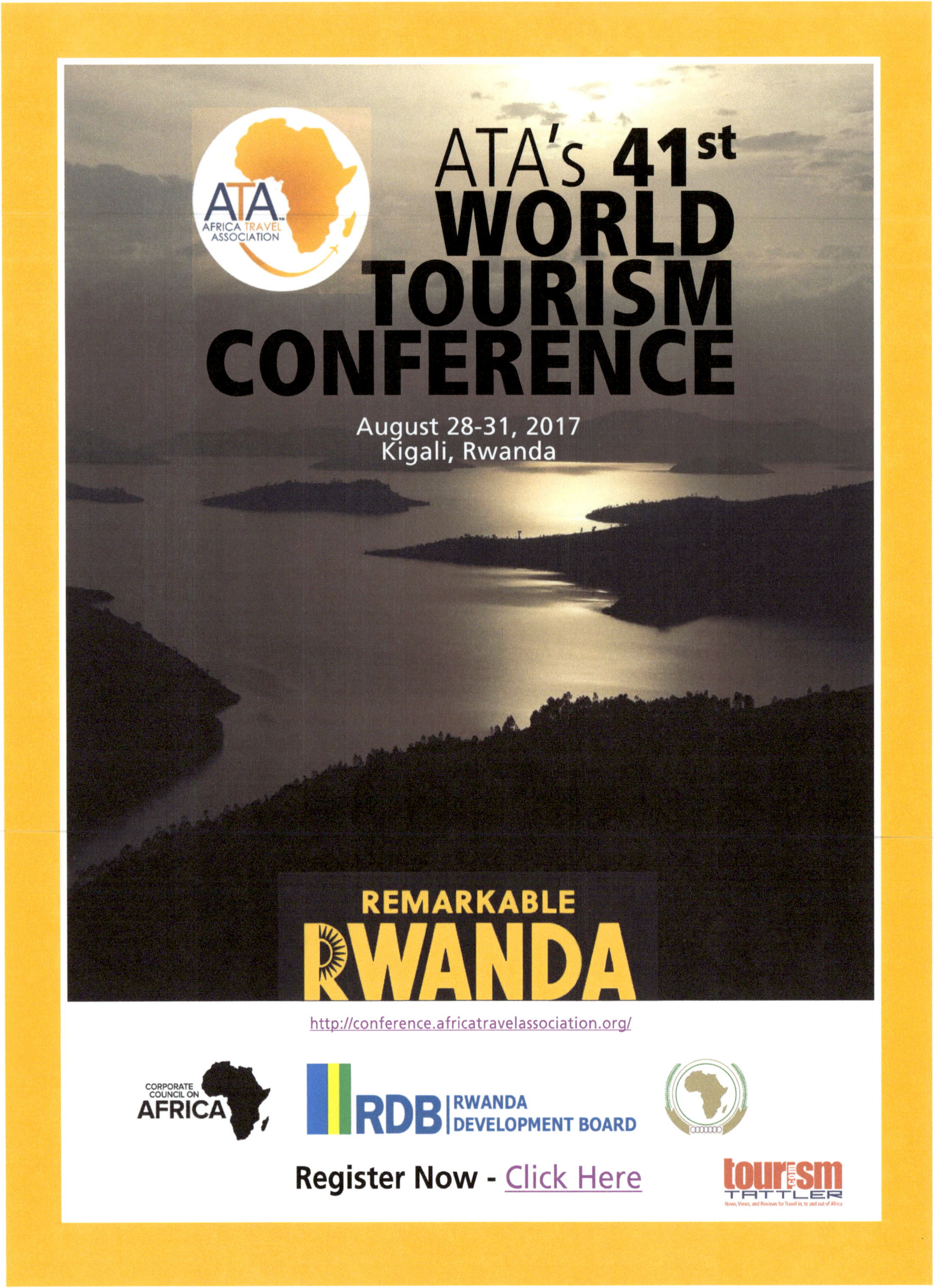

ATA's 41st WORLD TOURISM CONFERENCE

August 28-31, 2017
Kigali, Rwanda

REMARKABLE RWANDA

http://conference.africatravelassociation.org/

Register Now - Click Here

FROM THE BENCH
With Louis the Lawyer

The Consumer Goods & Services Ombudsman

Part 2

IMPLICATIONS FOR THE TOURISM INDUSTRY

THE CONSUMER GOODS & SERVICES OMBUDSMAN ('CGSO'), TERMS OF REFERENCE, POWERS & FUNCTIONS

The primary focus of the CGSO is to balance the rights and obligations of consumers and suppliers. As I have pointed out in earlier articles and workshops, it should be borne in mind is that there are in fact rights that accrue to suppliers and likewise consumers not only have rights but obligations too.

The CGSO is required to remain independent, objective, fair and equitable in applying the provisions of the Consumer Protection Act (CPA) and being an administrative body, as failure to act as aforesaid may well leave itself open to administrative law review.

The jurisdiction of the CGSO is subject to the following limitations:
- Claims must be brought within three years and the CGSO is required to advise consumers if the complaint lodged is older than two years.
- It must decline complaints that are unreasonable, frivolous, vexatious or if the complainant displays an offensive, threatening or abusive attitude.
- Likewise a matter may be declined if the CGSO is of the view that there does not appear to be a reasonable prospect of matter being settled.
- The complainant can at any time withdraw the complaint.
- If the matter is under consideration by a legal practitioner, the CGSO can decline involvement unless it feels the legal practitioner can add value.

Functions of the CGSO include the following:
- Investigate and evaluate the complaint to the extent that it contravenes the Code.
- Attempt to facilitate or make recommendations regarding settlement.
- If the parties have managed to settle the matter, the CGSO can upon request of the parties submit it to court/tribunal to be made a consent order – this may well be a good idea as any breach thereof by either party will be discouraged/be easier to enforce.
- Refer the matter to a more appropriate body.
- Make a recommendation/suggestion as to how the matter may be settled.

THE CGSO COMPLAINTS PROCESS

The CGSO Code encourages parties to resolve any disputes themselves, either amongst themselves or via the supplier's internal dispute mechanism. So much so that if the consumer goes directly to the CGSO, he will refer the consumer back to the supplier! However, it will not do so if it will result in *'undue hardship or inconvenience'* to the consumer – this is done when the consumer falls into the bracket of *'vulnerable'* consumers (See section 2 (1)(b) of the CPA).

However, the consumer may go to the CGSO if the consumer is dissatisfied with either the manner in which the supplier is dealing with the complaint or the outcome. Upon receipt of the complaint, the CGSO must check the time limits i.e. has the matter prescribed (brought too late) and whether it has jurisdiction. If the parties fail to resolve the matter themselves, the CGSO can either facilitate a settlement, mediate, or make a recommendation.

FACILITATION
- The code suggests that he can do so without conducting/carrying out an investigation which in itself is a bit mystifying!
- Nevertheless, he is obliged to gather *'all records and information'*.
- The CGSO may grant all, some or none of the remedies sought by the consumer and convey this to the parties.
- The parties can accept or reject it: if accepted it can be made a binding order and if rejected, the CGSO will advise them of other options.

MEDIATION
- The code once again indicates no investigation is required.
- It should be borne in mind that mediation is not binding.
- If the CGSO allows it, the parties may have legal representation.

RECOMMENDATION
- The recommendation by the CGSO must address the methodology and the give reasons.
- The CGSO can invite the comments of both parties.
- It must indicate who the CGSO believes to be liable, be it the retailer or wholesaler, if applicable.
- The recommendation, as with mediation, is not binding but if accepted by both parties (within the prescribed time limit), may be made an order of a court.
- If rejected, the CGSO will advise them of other options.

Disclaimer: This article is intended to provide a brief overview of legal matters pertaining to the tourism industry and is not intended as legal advice. © Adv Louis Nel, 'Louis The Lawyer', August 2017.